D1017537

Love

I love you

Love copyright © 2009 by Giles Andreae.
All rights reserved. Printed in China. No part of this book may be used or reproduced in any manner whatsoever without written permission except in the case of reprints in the context of reviews. For information, write Andrews McMeel Publishing, LLC, an Andrews McMeel Universal company, 1130 Walnut Street, Kansas City, Missouri 64106.

ISBN-13: 978-0-7407-7807-0
ISBN-10: 0-7407-7807-2

09 10 11 12 13 SDB 10 9 8 7 6 5 4 3 2 1

The author asserts the moral right to be identified as the author of this work.

www.edwardmonkton.com

www.andrewsmcmeel.com

ATTENTION: SCHOOLS AND BUSINESSES

Andrews McMeel books are available at quantity discounts with bulk purchase for educational, business, or sales promotional use. For information, please write to:
Special Sales Department, Andrews McMeel Publishing, LLC, 1130 Walnut Street, Kansas City, Missouri 64106.

LOVE

Edward Monkton

**Andrews McMeel
Publishing, LLC**

Kansas City • Sydney • London

You are like a wonderful LOVE CHOCOLATE – not one of the RUBBISH ones that nobody wants to eat but a REALLY NICE ONE that ALWAYS GOES FIRST!!

A LOVE CHOCOLATE

The LOVERS

Arm in arm they stand
on the SAUSAGE of LOVE
looking out together at the
KETCHUP of their DREAMS

Sometimes the HEART
should FOLLOW the MIND

Sometimes the HEART
should tell the MIND to
STAY AT HOME and
STOP INTERFERING

LOVE

you

me

go away you naughty enemies!

OK

us as biscuits

enemy biscuits

This picture of my DREAM shows how much I LOVE YOU*

* if you are not impressed by the biscuit thing PLEASE remember that it was only a DREAM

I LOVE you more than "THINGS"

Please understand that men have an **UNNATURAL PASSION** for non-living objects ("THINGS") So this is quite a **NICE** thing of me to say

Examples of "THINGS"

Frost-Free Refrigerator

Special Telescope

Sticky Tape Dispenser

Amazing "folding" car key

Hand Grenade

Submarine

The POTATO of LOVE

It is so full of LOVE that the ANGELS weep with envy at its coming and the HEAVENS sing a NEW and BEAUTEOUS song

I LOVE you SO MUCH that every night I shout out your BEAUTIFUL name to the distant STARS *

insert name here

*until the nice men come to take me away again

nee nor

COME DANCE into the STREETS

Come DANCE into the streets with me
For in the skies above
Shine the Brassiere of Fortune
And the Underpants of Love

My Darling

I LOVE you so much
that EVERYTHING
I look at makes me
think of YOU

The Kettle
of LOVE

The Teapot
of PASSION

The Toaster
of ATTRACTION

The Saucepan
of DESIRE

I WILL LOVE YOU...

Till the oceans run dry
Till the sea meets the sky
Till the fish learn to fly
Through a giant meat pie

INSIGNIFICANT MOMENTS when
I have LOVED you with ALL my HEART

Weds 8:03 am running through rain with bag on head
Sat 3:12 pm on bus next to "Mr Sweaty"
Thurs 11:53 am wiping "mayo" from "Turkey Mayo Sandwich" off shoes
Sun 4:12 am after being woken up by next door's cat (again)
Mon 9:13 am reading old mag at doctor's with all pages torn out except ad for Comfy Trousers
Tues 2:49 pm while on hold to person pretending "your call is important to us"
Fri 11:28 pm During Mutant Midgets TV documentary
Thurs 12:08 pm standing in endless line of morons at Post Office
This morning just after burning toast

I Love, Respect, Cherish, and Admire you for being the FREE and BEAUTIFUL and WONDERFUL Human Being that you are*

*except for when you're being
REALLY ANNOYING

LOVE MONKEY

FEEL his Lovely Love
surround you, for LOVE
is rare and precious - let
us TREASURE it all
we can